G000153551

CARPE DIEM

summersdale

CARPE DIEM

An Hachette UK Company
www.hachette.co.uk

Summersdale Publishers Ltd
Part of Octopus Publishing Group Limited
Carmelite House
50 Victoria Embankment
LONDON
EC4Y 0DZ
UK

www.summersdale.com

Printed and bound in the Czech Republic

ISBN: 978-1-78685-039-3

Substantial discounts on bulk quantities of Summersdale books are available to corporations, professional associations and other organisations. For details contact general enquiries: telephone: +44 (0) 1243 771107 or email: enquiries@summersdale.com.

Nov. 2018.

TO..Dariel.........................

FROM..Bernadette.....................
and Brian xxx

WHEN'S THE BEST TIME TO START? NOW!

THE ENVIOUS MOMENT
IS FLYING NOW, NOW,
WHILE WE'RE SPEAKING:
SEIZE THE DAY.

Horace

OPEN THE CURTAINS AND LET A NEW DAY BEGIN!

WITH THE NEW DAY COMES NEW STRENGTH AND NEW THOUGHTS.

Eleanor Roosevelt

You are never too old to set another goal or to dream a new dream.

Les Brown

BE A CHILD
AGAIN
TODAY,
AND SPREAD
SOME
MISCHIEF!

ACT AS IF WHAT
YOU DO MAKES
A DIFFERENCE.
IT DOES.

William James

OPPORTUNITIES MULTIPLY
AS THEY ARE SEIZED.

Sun Tzu

BUILD SOMETHING TODAY, HOWEVER SMALL.

I'd rather regret the things I've done than regret the things I haven't done.

Lucille Ball

IF YOU'RE GOING
THROUGH HELL,
KEEP GOING.

Winston Churchill

DIFFICULT DOESN'T MEAN IMPOSSIBLE.

IN THE MIDDLE OF DIFFICULTY LIES OPPORTUNITY.

Albert Einstein

One may walk over the highest mountain one step at a time.

John Wanamaker

SHARE THE FUN WHEREVER YOU GO TODAY.

**Wherever you are
– be all there.**

Jim Elliot

THINGS DO NOT
HAPPEN. THINGS ARE
MADE TO HAPPEN.

John F. Kennedy

TODAY IS A BLANK PAGE - WHAT ARE YOU GOING TO WRITE ON IT?

WHO SEEKS
SHALL FIND.

Sophocles

If you ask me what I came into this life to do, I will tell you: I came to live out loud.

Émile Zola

GOOD THINGS COME TO THOSE WHO... GO OUT AND GET THEM!

FOR MYSELF, I AM AN OPTIMIST... IT DOES NOT SEEM TO BE MUCH USE BEING **ANYTHING ELSE.**

Winston Churchill

Whenever you fall, pick something up.

Oswald Avery

EVERY CHANGE BRINGS OPPORTUNITY WITH IT.

EITHER YOU RUN THE
DAY OR THE DAY
RUNS YOU.

Jim Rohn

TELL ME, WHAT IS IT
YOU PLAN TO DO WITH
YOUR ONE WILD AND
PRECIOUS LIFE?

Mary Oliver

LIFE IS ABOUT TAKING PART.

Expect problems and eat them for breakfast.

Alfred A. Montapert

THE MOST EFFECTIVE WAY
TO DO IT, IS TO DO IT.

Amelia Earhart

MAKE IT
HAPPEN!

TURN YOUR FACE
TO THE SUN AND
THE SHADOWS FALL
BEHIND YOU.

Maori proverb

To know oneself, one should assert oneself.

Albert Camus

LISTEN TO YOUR INNER VOICE.

I CAN,
THEREFORE **I AM.**

Simone Weil

**In order to succeed,
we must first believe
that we can.**

Nikos Kazantzakis

YOU ARE THE HERO OF YOUR STORY.

YOU MUST BE
THE CHANGE YOU
WISH TO SEE IN
THE WORLD.

Mahatma Gandhi

LIFE IS SIMPLE,
IT'S JUST **NOT EASY.**

Anonymous

WHAT ARE YOU WAITING FOR?

All life is an experiment. The more experiments you make, the better.

Ralph Waldo Emerson

NO ONE KNOWS WHAT HE
CAN DO TILL HE TRIES.

Publilius Syrus

MAKE A WISH... THEN MAKE IT COME TRUE!

LIFE IS A SHIPWRECK,
BUT WE MUST NOT
FORGET TO SING IN
THE LIFEBOATS.

Voltaire

Whether you think you can or you think you can't, you're right.

Henry Ford

WHO'S THAT IN THE MIRROR? LOOKS LIKE A GO-GETTER TO ME.

LIFE ISN'T ABOUT FINDING
YOURSELF. LIFE IS ABOUT
CREATING YOURSELF.

George Bernard Shaw

**Do what you can,
with what you have,
where you are.**

Theodore Roosevelt

WHEN LIFE

THROWS

TOMATOES

AT YOU,

MAKE A

BLOODY

MARY!

WHEN YOU REACH
THE END OF YOUR
ROPE, TIE A KNOT IN
IT AND HANG ON.

Anonymous

PERSEVERANCE IS
FAILING NINETEEN TIMES
AND SUCCEEDING
THE TWENTIETH.

Julie Andrews

YOU
ONLY
LIVE
ONCE.

Opportunity does not knock, it presents itself when you beat down the door.

Kyle Chandler

BEGIN TO BE NOW WHAT
YOU WILL BE HEREAFTER.

William James

SQUEEZE ALL THE JUICE OUT OF TODAY!

SET YOUR GOALS
HIGH, AND DON'T
STOP TILL YOU
GET THERE.

Bo Jackson

Nothing is a waste of time if you use the experience wisely.

Auguste Rodin

YOUR LIFE
IS A WORK
OF ART – IT
DESERVES
TO BE SEEN.

FIND ECSTASY IN LIFE;
THE MERE SENSE OF
LIVING IS **JOY ENOUGH.**

Emily Dickinson

It's always too early to quit.

Norman Vincent Peale

DON'T RACE FOR THE FINISH LINE: ENJOY THE JOURNEY.

IF YOU WAIT, ALL
THAT HAPPENS
IS THAT YOU
GET OLDER.

Mario Andretti

ONE JOY SCATTERS
A HUNDRED GRIEFS.

Chinese proverb

MAKE
EVERY
MINUTE
COUNT.

How wonderful it is
that nobody need wait
a single moment before
starting to improve
the world.

Anne Frank

IT'S OK TO HAVE
BUTTERFLIES IN YOUR
STOMACH. JUST GET THEM
TO FLY IN FORMATION.

Rob Gilbert

GRAB A
DOUBLE
HELPING
OF LIFE,
WITH A SIDE
ORDER OF
ADVENTURE.

LIFE IS EITHER A
DARING ADVENTURE
OR NOTHING.

Helen Keller

Opportunities are like sunrises. If you wait too long, you miss them.

William Arthur Ward

LIFE IS SWEET: TAKE A BIG BITE!

THERE ARE
ALWAYS FLOWERS
FOR THOSE WHO
WANT TO **SEE THEM.**

Henri Matisse

You're the blacksmith of your own happiness.

Swedish proverb

TO REST
IS TO RUST:
STAY SHINY
AND BRIGHT!

WE ARE ALL IN THE
GUTTER, BUT SOME
OF US ARE LOOKING
AT THE STARS.

Oscar Wilde

SOME DAYS THERE WON'T
BE A SONG IN YOUR
HEART. **SING ANYWAY.**

Emory Austin

SING A SONG,
PAINT A
PICTURE...
CHANGE THE
WORLD.

Live the questions now. Perhaps you will then gradually, without noticing it, live along some distant day into the answer.

Rainer Maria Rilke

THE SECRET OF
GETTING AHEAD IS
GETTING STARTED.

Mark Twain

EVERY DAWN IS A NEW BEGINNING, A TIME TO START A NEW STORY.

Setting goals is the first step in turning the invisible into the visible.

Tony Robbins

THE WISE DOES AT ONCE WHAT THE FOOL DOES AT LAST.

Baltasar Gracián

WHY WATCH TV WHEN REAL LIFE IS SO MUCH MORE EXCITING?

YOU CAN'T USE UP
CREATIVITY. THE MORE YOU
USE, THE **MORE YOU HAVE.**

Maya Angelou

LIVE TODAY, FOR TOMORROW IT WILL ALL BE HISTORY.

Proverb

KEEP CALM

AND SEIZE

THE DAY.

If you can find a
path with no obstacles,
it probably doesn't
lead anywhere.

Frank A. Clark

BE HAPPY.
IT'S ONE WAY OF
BEING WISE.

Colette

LIVE
YOUR
DREAMS.

IT IS NEVER TOO LATE
TO BE WHAT YOU
MIGHT HAVE BEEN.

Adelaide Anne Procter

A JOURNEY OF A
THOUSAND MILES
BEGINS WITH A
SINGLE STEP.

Lao Tzu

**LIVE LIFE
OFF THE MAP
AND BE
YOUR OWN
COMPASS.**

**The best way to
predict the future
is to create it.**

Abraham Lincoln

EVERY ARTIST WAS
FIRST AN AMATEUR.

Ralph Waldo Emerson

TALK TO SOMEONE NEW. YOU COULD MAKE THEIR DAY — AND THEY MIGHT MAKE YOURS.

I HAVE NEVER MET A
MAN SO IGNORANT
THAT I COULDN'T LEARN
SOMETHING FROM HIM.

Galileo Galilei

TO ME, EVERY
HOUR OF THE DAY
AND NIGHT IS AN
UNSPEAKABLY
PERFECT MIRACLE.

Walt Whitman

YOU ARE
A SONG —
MAKE SURE
YOU'RE
HEARD.

Life shrinks or expands in proportion to one's courage.

Anaïs Nin

THE BEST WAY TO MAKE
YOUR DREAMS COME TRUE
IS TO **WAKE UP.**

Paul Valéry

LOOK AT LIFE FROM UNEXPECTED ANGLES TODAY.

TO SUCCEED IN
LIFE, YOU NEED
THREE THINGS:
A WISHBONE,
A BACKBONE AND
A FUNNY BONE.

Reba McEntire

LIFE IS A HELLUVA LOT
MORE FUN IF YOU SAY
'YES' RATHER THAN 'NO'.

Richard Branson

BE WHO YOU'VE ALWAYS WANTED TO BE.

Look at life through the windshield, not the rear-view mirror.

Byrd Baggett

THE BEST WAY OUT IS ALWAYS THROUGH.

Robert Frost

MAKE YOUR OWN SUNSHINE.

LOOK AT EVERYTHING
AS THOUGH YOU WERE
SEEING IT FOR THE
FIRST OR **LAST TIME.**

Betty Smith

THE MAN WHO REMOVES A MOUNTAIN BEGINS BY CARRYING AWAY SMALL STONES.

Chinese proverb

YOU CAN
DO IT.
ALL YOU
HAVE TO DO
IS TRY.

Nothing really matters except what you do now in this instant of time.

Eileen Caddy

IF YOUR SHIP
DOESN'T COME IN,
SWIM OUT TO IT.

Jonathan Winters

JUST BE
YOURSELF.

THERE ARE EXACTLY
AS MANY SPECIAL
OCCASIONS IN LIFE
AS WE CHOOSE
TO CELEBRATE.

Robert Brault

LIFE BEGINS AT
THE END OF YOUR
COMFORT ZONE.

Neale Donald Walsch

LIFE IS NOT A REHEARSAL ENJOY THE LIMELIGHT!

Most folks are as happy as they make up their minds to be.

Abraham Lincoln

I HAVE FOUND THAT
IF YOU LOVE LIFE, LIFE
WILL LOVE YOU BACK.

Arthur Rubinstein

IF YOU'RE ALREADY
WALKING ON THIN
ICE, YOU MIGHT AS
WELL DANCE.

Proverb

I COULDN'T WAIT FOR
SUCCESS, SO I WENT
AHEAD **WITHOUT IT.**

Jonathan Winters

GO AND
GET IT!

You can have anything
you want if you will
give up the belief that
you can't have it.

Robert Anthony

WHEN IT IS DARKEST,
MEN SEE THE STARS.

Ralph Waldo Emerson

NOBODY CAN HOLD YOU BACK.

YOU CAN'T EXPECT TO
HIT THE JACKPOT IF YOU
DON'T PUT A FEW NICKELS
IN THE MACHINE.

Flip Wilson

Change your life today. Don't gamble on the future, act now, without delay.

Simone de Beauvoir

SHOW THE WORLD WHAT YOU'RE MADE OF.

LIFE ISN'T ABOUT WAITING
FOR THE STORM TO PASS;
IT'S ABOUT LEARNING TO
DANCE IN THE RAIN.

Anonymous

SHOOT FOR THE
MOON. EVEN IF YOU
MISS, YOU'LL LAND
AMONG THE STARS.

Les Brown

DRESS TO IMPRESS AND BE THE BEST YOU CAN BE.

Don't get your knickers in a knot. Nothing is solved and it just makes you walk funny.

Kathryn Carpenter

HAPPINESS IS A WAY
OF TRAVEL, NOT A
DESTINATION.

Roy M. Goodman

YOU'RE NEVER LOST – YOU'RE JUST DISCOVERING NEW PLACES.

Opportunity is missed by most people because it is dressed in overalls and looks like work.

Thomas Edison

DIFFICULTIES STRENGTHEN THE MIND, AS LABOUR DOES **THE BODY.**

Seneca the Younger

TURN YOUR HOPES INTO REALITIES.

OUR GREATEST GLORY IS
NOT IN NEVER FALLING,
BUT IN RISING EVERY
TIME WE FALL.

Confucius

**First say to yourself
what you would be;
and then do what
you have to do.**

Epictetus

MAKE AN IMPRESSION!

LUCK IS A DIVIDEND
OF SWEAT. THE MORE
YOU SWEAT, THE
LUCKIER YOU GET.

Ray Kroc

DON'T LOAF AND
INVITE INSPIRATION;
LIGHT OUT AFTER IT
WITH A CLUB.

Jack London

WELCOME
TODAY'S
CHALLENGES.

When you come to a roadblock, take a detour.

Mary Kay Ash

THE SEASON OF FAILURE IS THE BEST TIME FOR SOWING THE SEEDS **OF SUCCESS.**

Paramahansa Yogananda

SPOT THE FLOWERS THAT GROW UP THROUGH THE CRACKS.

It's never too late –
never too late to start
over, never too late
to be happy.

Jane Fonda

IF THE WIND WILL
NOT SERVE, TAKE
TO THE OARS.

Latin proverb

BE A GIFT
TO THE WORLD
TODAY.

YOU CAN'T TURN BACK
THE CLOCK BUT YOU CAN
WIND IT UP AGAIN.

Bonnie Prudden

THE PURPOSE
OF OUR LIVES IS
TO BE HAPPY.

Dalai Lama

DOORS ARE MADE TO BE OPENED; LOCKS ARE MADE TO FIT A KEY.

What matters is to live in the present, live now, for every moment is now.

Sathya Sai Baba

WHOEVER IS
HAPPY WILL MAKE
OTHERS HAPPY TOO.

Anne Frank

MAKE NEW CONNECTIONS TODAY!

A MIND IS LIKE
A PARACHUTE.
IT DOESN'T WORK
IF IT IS NOT OPEN.

Frank Zappa

WITH THE PAST,
I HAVE NOTHING TO DO;
NOR WITH THE FUTURE.
I LIVE NOW.

Ralph Waldo Emerson

CARPE
DIEM.

If you're interested in finding out more about our books, find us on Facebook at **Summersdale Publishers** and follow us on Twitter at **@Summersdale**.

www.summersdale.com